Games We Play

Ellen Lawrence

LIGHTBOX

Go to
www.openlightbox.com
and enter this book's
unique code.

ACCESS CODE

LBS75522

Lightbox is an all-inclusive digital solution for the teaching and learning of curriculum topics in an original, groundbreaking way. Lightbox is based on National Curriculum Standards.

OPTIMIZED FOR

- ✓ **TABLETS**
- ✓ **WHITEBOARDS**
- ✓ **COMPUTERS**
- ✓ **AND MUCH MORE!**

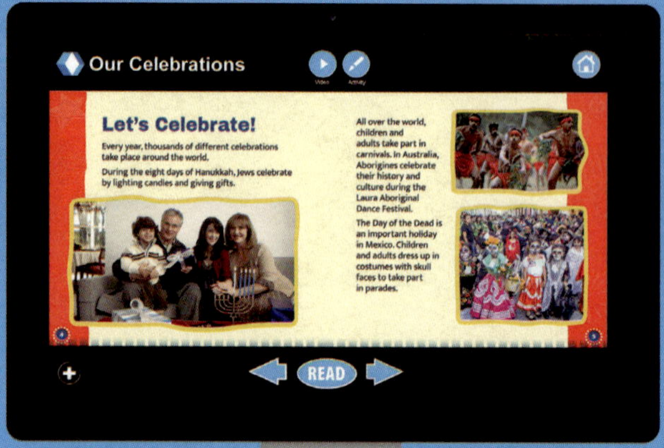

STANDARD FEATURES OF LIGHTBOX

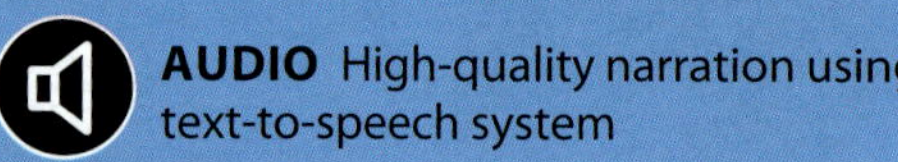

AUDIO High-quality narration using text-to-speech system

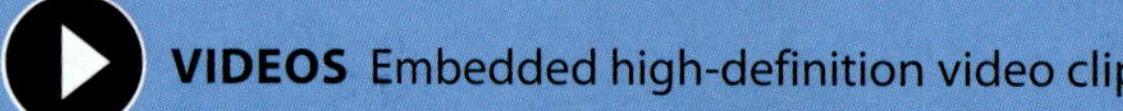

VIDEOS Embedded high-definition video clips

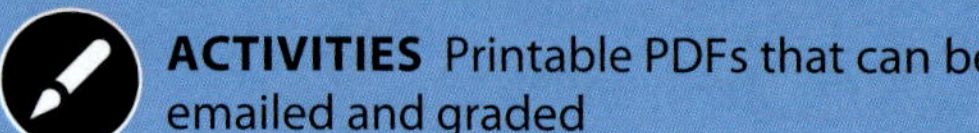

ACTIVITIES Printable PDFs that can be emailed and graded

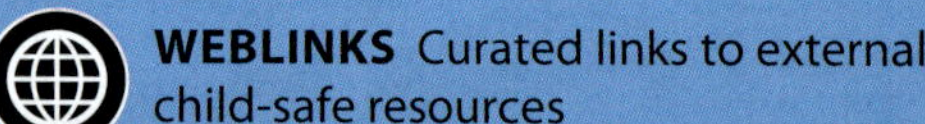

WEBLINKS Curated links to external, child-safe resources

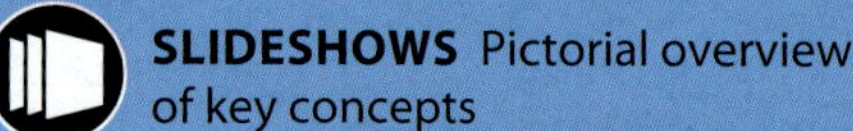

SLIDESHOWS Pictorial overviews of key concepts

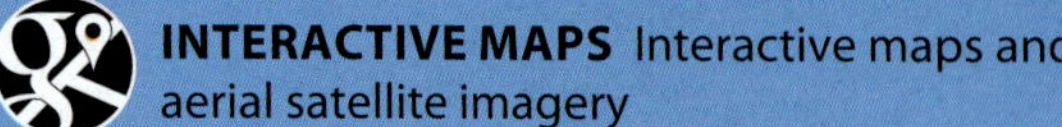

INTERACTIVE MAPS Interactive maps and aerial satellite imagery

QUIZ **QUIZZES** Ten multiple choice questions that are automatically graded and emailed for teacher assessment

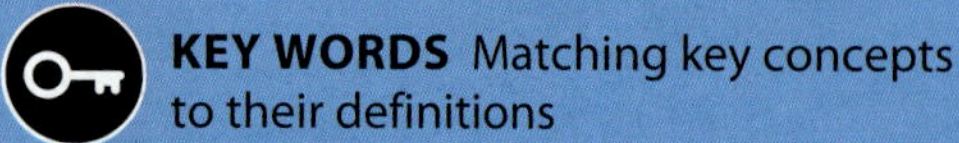

KEY WORDS Matching key concepts to their definitions

VIDEOS

WEBLINKS

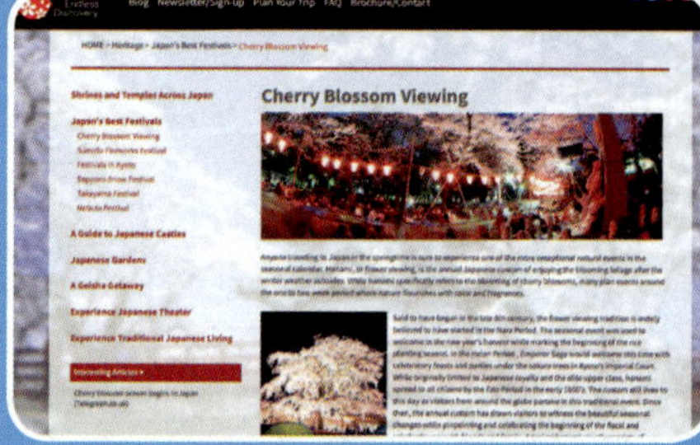

SLIDESHOWS

QUIZZES

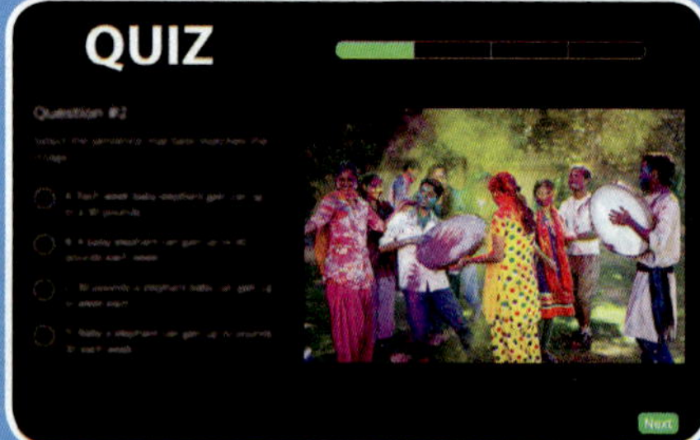

About Our World

Games We Play

It's Time to Play!

In Thailand, jumping rope is a popular game. Children make their own long ropes by looping lots of rubber bands together.

In the United States, a playground, a broom handle, and a tennis ball are all that's needed for a game of stickball.

In France, boys and girls hold on tight to playground merry-go-rounds.

Kids and teenagers in Ethiopia enjoy outdoor games of foosball.

Taking turns at wheelbarrow rides is great fun for many kids in Vietnam.

A Game of Soccer

All around the world, kids love to play soccer.

Many children live in poverty, though. Their families cannot afford to buy them soccer balls.

For some soccer-crazy boys and girls, that's not a problem. These inventive young players make their own soccer balls from plastic bags!

Many people call Madrid, Spain, the Soccer Capital of the World.

One way to make a soccer ball is to pack scrunched-up newspaper inside a plastic bag. Then the first bag is covered with up to 30 more plastic bags. Finally, the ball of bags is held together with rubber bands, string, or strips of old cloth.

Riding a Bike

Riding a bike is a popular pastime for children all over the world.

In many parts of Africa, kids and adults ride bikes made of wood. These tough, wooden bikes are used for more than just having fun.

The bikes are also used to carry goods such as fruit, vegetables, and firewood.

Wooden bikes don't have pedals. The rider sits or stands on the bike and pushes along the ground with his or her feet.

Rolling Tires

An old tire might look like a piece of junk. It can easily become a fun new toy, though.

In many parts of the world, children look for old tires in garbage dumps. Then they have fun rolling and chasing their tires. Kids compete to see who can roll their tire the fastest and farthest.

You have to be in good shape to run alongside a fast-moving tire. It also takes skill to keep the tire rolling or make it change direction. Many kids use sticks to control their tires.

It's Fun to Swing

Up and down. Up and down. All over the world, kids love to play on swings.

You can swing on an old tire. You can swing in a playground.

Baka children live in a rainforest in Cameroon. They make their swings out of liana vines.

Liana vines are plants with long, thin, bendy stems. The vines grow up from the ground and get tangled in trees. Then the vines dangle back down from the tree branches like ropes and are great for swinging!

The world record for the longest time swinging on a swing is 32 hours.

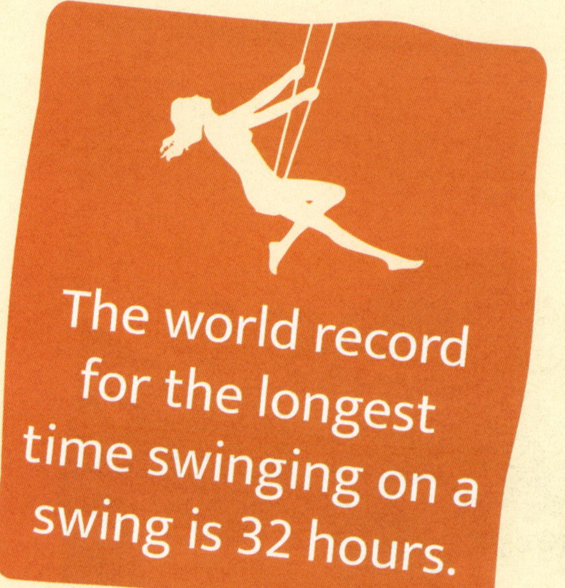

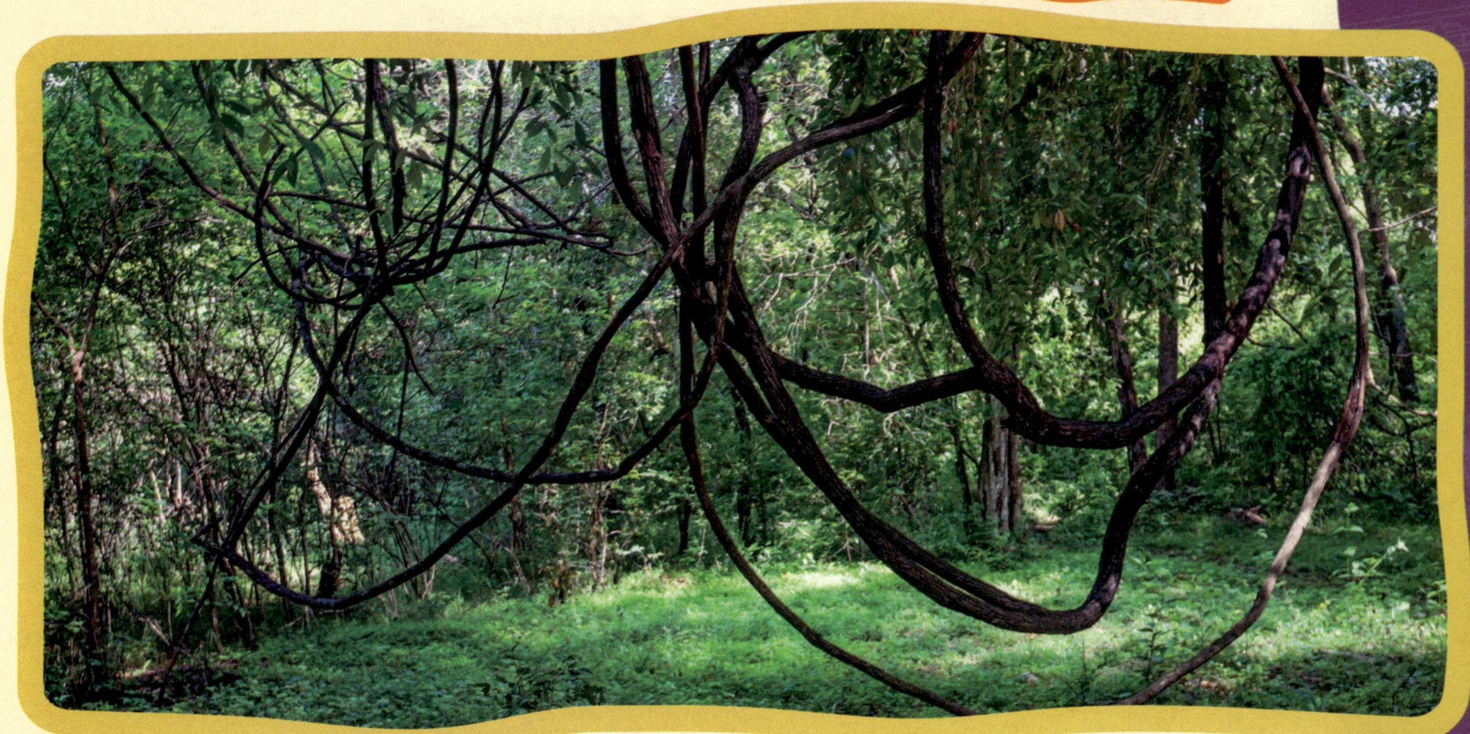

Let's Play Tug-of-War

Tug-of-war is played in nearly every part of the world. In Vietnam, it has been a traditional contest for centuries.

To win a game, one team must pull the other team over a line drawn on the ground.

Tug-of-war teams usually pull on a rope. Sometimes, however, children have no rope. Then they just hold onto each other and pull hard!

There's no limit to how many players can join in a game of tug-of-war. Each team might have just two or three players or as many as ten!

Kite Fighting and Running

In Afghanistan, people love to fly kites and take part in kite fighting. During a kite fight, competitors try to cut the string of their opponent's kite.

The strings of fighter kites are covered with tiny pieces of crushed glass. This helps the strings cut through the strings of other kites. The loser's kite then floats off.

Kids and grown-ups chase after kites that have been cut free. This is called kite running. The kite runner who catches a free kite gets to keep it!

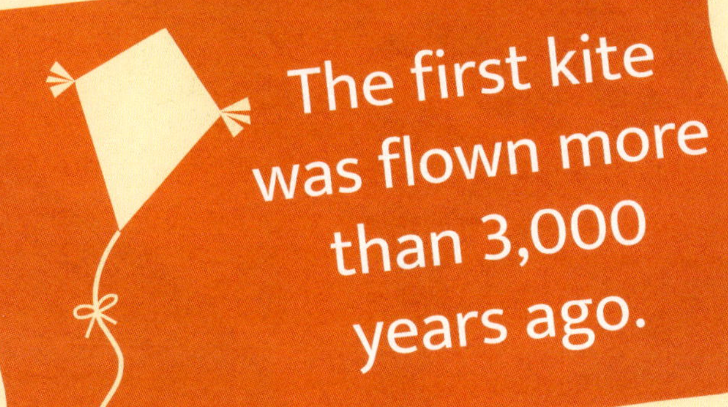

Winning Rubber Bands

In many parts of Southeast Asia, children like to play a game with rubber bands.

Each player places a rubber band on the ground. Then the players begin blowing on their rubber bands.

The object of the game is to blow your rubber band on top of your opponent's.

The winner of a game gets to keep both rubber bands.

Blowing a rubber band to an exact spot isn't easy. Players have to control the direction and speed of the air they blow out. Young players learn their skills by watching older kids and getting lots of practice.

Our Favorite Toys

All over the world, children play with their favorite toys.

The toys may look very different, but they are all the same in one important way—kids love them!

12

What is your favorite game? How is it like these games? How is it different?

How do the places kids live change the games they play?

KEY WORDS

Research has shown that as much as 65 percent of all written material published in English is made up of 300 words. These 300 words cannot be taught using pictures or learned by sounding them out. They must be recognized by sight. This book contains 127 common sight words to help young readers improve their reading fluency and comprehension. This book also teaches young readers several important content words, such as proper nouns. These words are paired with pictures to aid in learning and improve understanding.

Page	Sight Words First Appearance
4	a, all, and, are, boys, by, children, for, girls, go, in, is, it's, long, make, of, on, own, play, states, the, their, time, to, together
5	at, great, many, turns
6	around, from, live, not, some, them, these, world, young
7	call, first, more, old, one, or, people, then, up, way, with
8	over
9	along, also, as, carry, don't, feet, goods, have, her, his, just, made, parts, such, than, used
10	an, can, it, like, look, might, new, see, they, who
11	be, change, keep, run, takes, you
12	down, out
13	back, get, grow, plants, trees
14	been, each, every, hard, has, line, must, no, other, sometimes
15	how, three, two
16	cut, try
17	after, helps, off, that, this, through, was, years
18	begin, places, your
19	air, both, learn
20	but, different, important, may, our, same, very
22	what
23	do

Page	Content Words First Appearance
4	broom, children, France, game, merry-go-rounds, playground, rope, rubber bands, stickball, tennis, Thailand
5	Ethiopia, foosball, teenagers, Vietnam, wheelbarrow
6	bags, plastic, poverty, soccer
7	capital, cloth, Madrid, newspaper, Spain, string
8	bike
9	adults, Africa, firewood, fruit, ground, kids, pedals, rider, vegetables, wood
10	garbage dumps, junk, tires
11	sticks
12	Baka, Cameroon, liana vines, swings
13	branches, stems
16	Afghanistan, competitors, kite
17	glass
18	Southeast Asia

Published by Smartbook Media Inc.
350 5th Avenue, 59th Floor New York, NY 10118
Website: www.openlightbox.com

Printed in the United States of America in Brainerd, Minnesota
1 2 3 4 5 6 7 8 9 0 22 21 20 19 18

012018
120117

Library of Congress Cataloging in Publication Control Number: 2017959805

ISBN 978-1-5105-3546-6 (hardcover)
ISBN 978-1-5105-3547-3 (multi-user eBook)

Project Coordinator: John Willis
Art Director: Terry Paulhus

Every reasonable effort has been made to trace ownership and to obtain permission to reprint copyright material. The publisher would be pleased to have any errors or omissions brought to its attention so that they may be corrected in subsequent printings.
The publisher acknowledges Getty Images and Alamy as its primary image suppliers for this title.